LIFE IN THE MOMENT

A collection of short poems, and
inspirational words

From one Man's Journey in The Here and Now

By
STEVEN CLAGUE

Copyright © 2022 by Steven Clague

All rights reserved. No part of this book may be reproduced or used in any manner without written permission of the copyright owner except for the use of quotations in a book review. For more information: stephenclagueauthor@gmail.com

FIRST EDITION

ISBNs:

Paperback: 978-1-80227-334-2

eBook: 978-1-80227-335-9

Contents

Chapter 1: In The Now 5

Chapter 2: Nature 83

Chapter 3: Love 123

Chapter 4: Live Life Give Thanks 143

Chapter 5: Death 169

Chapter 1
In The Now

Nothing to know

Watching waves on a coastal cliff,

Peace and quiet on a hill,

Lying down fluffy clouds,

Sitting under a mighty tree.

Looking at flowers, buzzing bees

In a park, on a summers day.

There are no questions at times like these,

Nothing that needs to be known;

Only a presence that's always there, always was, and will be forever more.

Holy Ground;

The place where we stand is holy ground.

All is sacred, you and me,

Life is special, so divine,

Tiny any, mighty tree

So full of mystery.

Don't get stuck in dull routines,

See the beauty all around,

A stranger's smile, a fluffy cloud.

Heaven isn't way out there,

It's here and now, so be aware.

Be

Just be, simplicity

Not changing, or rearranging,

Or looking for experience.

Life in motion

Here and now,

Deep breath,

Feel alive.

Nowhere to go,

Nothing to do,

Just be.

Don't fight

When the dark grey cloud comes upon you

Don't let it take over; say 'hello' and let it flow,

Try not to pass it on.

Treat the sadness and gloom like an old friend,

nothing lasts forever.

Stay aware, and stand alert,

Don't let it turn to anger or hate;

In no time the cloud will pass

Then brightness will return.

Here and Now

Here and now, all is as it should be.

Here and now, life moves along to its rhythm of old.

Here and now, I am doing nothing, life it happens to me.

Here and now, change is all around, and also new beginnings.

Here and now, the moment is so unique, once in a lifetime, won't come again.

Here and now, life is all there is, and all there ever can be is life.

Here and now, all is good, nothing more to say.

Who am I?

Who is that staring back at myself in the mirror?

Is it me, you, or could it be the universe?

How or why, I have this body, I do not know.

All I do know is that I exist, and I will still be here when this body goes.

I am not on this short trip through space and time, to live in pain or fear,

But here to live and discover the wonder of life, and awaken to the oneness and love of all.

I am

Can't plan for a future, when it's just in the mind.

Life is always now; you will find

The next breath is promised to no one,

Not me or you, or any living thing, can be taken away before you blink.

Enjoy the moment, it's all we have

because all I know, is that I am.

Open

Shh, be still be quiet,

Look what's about, all is new

Here and now.

Mystery is at your door, open up,

Let the world say 'hello'.

Too busy

Busy, being busy and not aware,

Mind it races, here and there.

Stop for a moment, take a breath, make no sound,

Feel the earth, beneath my feet.

Be aware of how calm and still our earth is.

Any questions and answers I may have,

They evaporate, like puddles of water, on a summer's day,

There is nothing I need to know.

All that remains is a silence beyond any sound I can hear,

And a peace no words can explain,

From chaos to harmony, by just being aware.

Sit

Just sit and be quiet,

Look within; leave the mind alone,

Let the thoughts come and go

Like drops of rain on your windowpane.

When the mind is still

What remains?

Just love, peace and joy,

That is all.

Eternity

As you are reading this, be aware

That this moment is eternity,

All that there is

Flying through the heavens

On our good ship, called earth.

You may be feeling restless and bored,

Slightly annoyed, but relax and remember

That you hold eternity, in the palm of your hand.

Life coming at you

Talking to a stranger about the weather, say goodbye move on, moment gone.

A pigeon is walking next to me, gone, move on.

A smile from a lady in the street,

Look up, gulls circling up above, making beautiful noise.

Say 'hello' to a couple holding hands, moment gone, move on,

Stop to tie my shoelace, a work of art on the lamppost,

Did the spider create that just for me?

Walk on, the wind on my face, something flies in front of me,

Gone, move on. Everything goes from light to dark,

Look up, a big fluffy cloud covers the sun.

A feather floats down from the sky,

A tall man says 'hello', life is coming at me thick and fast.

Its light again, the cloud has moved on,

Everything seems to constantly change,

Hear a rook, a car and a gull,

Never a dull moment, when you're aware.
A tree is dancing being blown by the wind,
A toddler is in a pram, eyes everywhere loving life;
That was us long ago, a blank slate at one with the world.
The child is still with us, when we see the miracles
In what we call ordinary life.

Bad Weather?

"Hello my friend how are you"

"Ok I guess, but sick to death, of this bloody miserable weather!"

"Sorry my friend, I have to disagree, this is the greatest day there ever was!"

"What do you mean? Its damp and its grey"

"Well you are alive and so am I, we have been blessed with another day, each day is a miracle, when your alive"

"When you put it like that you are correct"

"Life is to short to waste it away, enjoy life my friend and have a great day!"

Stuck

Is this life, a moment, this moment presenting itself to you,

And passing through you? An invisible energy

Constantly flowing, like a river always changing and forever new.

What happens when you grab the moment

And it does not pass through?

You're not aware, and are stuck in the past or the future,

Locked in a world, of fear, negativity and worry,

More a swamp than a free, flowing river,

Then you miss out on the wonder each moment brings, the miracle of life,

A chance to be reborn in each new moment.

Creation is now and Eden is near,

So let each moment pass through, and then the next.

Don't get caught in the dramas of life,

Be reborn here and now, let life flow,

Don't be a puddle cut off from the source.

Arise

The time is now, to wake from sleep,

Missing the moment again and again,

Spending our days, self-absorbed, in tunnel vision,

Unaware of the deeper life, missing the sacred in all we see.

Using our mind, which reads the news,

Singing the same song, reacting to events as we always do.

When life is forever changing, it is time for us to change our ways,

Plant a seed within our souls, watch it grow and flower with love,

Say thanks; when things they go wrong,

Stop and look around now and then,

Try and pause before you react, see the mystery in every event.

Get out of your mind, and enter the heart,

Quit being the caterpillar, seeing the world as you always have,

And soar like the butterfly; see the wonder of life,

A new song will be played, in your heart
And your inner garden will be in bloom.

Am I here?

Am I here, or am I everywhere?

When the mind is restless, believing in little old me,

Then I am here, alone and afraid,

When the mind is still and at peace,

I am one with all that I see,

Limitless and forever free.

A simple smile

Who says a smile can't change the world?

A heroin addict walking the streets

Been clean for about 3 weeks,

Trying so hard not to shoot,

Can't take no more, got to score.

See a stranger on his way,

A big smile and friendly 'hello'.

Something changes in his brain,

Goes to shop to buy food for his boy,

A world has changed for the better this day,

With the power of a smile, and a friendly 'hello'.

Overtake

Watching a bird glide up in the heavens

Until it disappears from my eyes.

Just 10 seconds, and no more,

My thoughts, they have flown away.

Mind so calm and so true,

So simple, easy to do.

Try this a few times a day.

Peace it overtakes my restless mind,

I then feel free, just like the birds up in the sky.

What do we need?

What do we truly need for our day, today?
A little food and water to keep us going,
Some knowledge for the tasks we need to do,
Love and understanding, for the people we meet,
Nothing we need for ourselves,
All is done by the invisible hand
That loves and nourishes all the land.
Don't let your mind make it complicated;
Life is simple, best to walk the humble path.

Inside and out

The inside thing that I am,

And the outside thing that I see,

Is there any difference?

Or are they one and the same?

Could it be, that what you see is inside you?

And you are in all that you see?

If you see yourself, separate from the world,

Then you will not be in all that you see;

But if you stop and be still,

Maybe, just maybe, you will see yourself

In the flowers, the birds and the bees.

Attention

How well, do we truly know each other?

Our mothers and brothers, lovers, family and our friends.

How often do we truly listen with our full attention?

Not absorbed in our own private world, one eye on something else.

Try and see, how different it feels,

When you talk or hug, with complete attention,

Alive and aware of the moment.

See how different it feels when truly aware.

Come back

To see yourself in the other,

And to see the other in yourself

Is it how it is meant to be?

The end of fear, and despair,

We are all the same you and I;

The sun shines, on everyone,

Old and young, rich and poor.

The rain, pours down on everyone,

No one is ever truly alone,

We are all that we see,

The universe is us, here and now,

Let's stop pretending, and come back to our true home.

Shadows

Shadows moving, along the ground

Here then gone, don't hang around.

My own shadow follows me

Hide and seek, through the day.

Something in the way of light,

That is why shadows are not bright.

Look at my shadow, think of life,

What part, of me stops the light,

My inner lamp, from shining bright?

Fear or anger, jealousy or greed?

Look at myself with open heart,

Remove the blockage which stops the light,

So I can see the glory that life is,

Then let the world see my glow.

Simple

Throwing a stone into the river,

Watching a feather float to the ground,

Kicking a ball in the park,

Sitting down on a summer's day,

Talking with friends, lots of hugs,

A cup of tea, walking the dog.

I think it's always been this way;

Simple things in this life are the best.

A bin

Sunday morning, few hours work,
Emptying bins, all is good.
Blocking a road, to get to a bin,
Man in car, wants to pass.
Only a moment, won't take long.
Man, he rages, just can't wait;
Feel his anger, sense his rage,
Bad energy, just calm down.
Shouts at me, hurls abuse,
I feel calm, hurting himself more than me,
Get in cab, driver asks, what's going on?
He gets angry, full of rage,
Gets out the cab, to confront the man.
Fingers pointed; words exchanged,
Negative emotions in their bloodstream.
Me in the cab nice and chilled,
Calm down boys it's only a bin,

Let it go, and let it flow,

All is well in the world.

The sun is still in the sky, and you are still alive!

Excited

I went for a walk to get ink on my arm,

Summers day, scent of flowers in the air,

Cry of a falcon fills the sky,

Good vibes are all around.

Hear a robin sing his song.

Won't be long till I'm in the chair

Say 'hello' to people that I see,

A baby looks and smiles at me,

Get to the tattoo shop, only to be told

'Sorry pal I'm doubled booked, so sorry about that'.

Emotion stirs deep within, but then subsides with a grin.

'Thank you,' I say, all meant to be,

Beautiful walk, unique just for me,

No other on earth, has seen what I just saw,

I guess it was not meant to be.

What's it all about?

What is the meaning of this life, what's the meaning of you and me?

What is the meaning of a flea?

Could it be, that we are just here now, living in this unstoppable moment,

Being carried along by the dance of life,

The waves of the sea dancing and waving at us,

The trees swaying to and frow, the cry of the gull,

The rain dancing as it hits the ground, children playing with the energy of life.

What happens when you forget the dance, lost in the drama of the world?

Planning for a future that may never come,

Working and saving for the dream car, house or holiday;

Desires fulfilled leading to more and more desires,

Trying to find answers about the meaning of life.

What's it all about, this life? Is there a God?

Why are we here, do we go to heaven?

Some may say reincarnation is the way,

More confusion in the minds of man;

Could it be, that we are just here now, and so is the flea,

And life is a dance done in the here and now,

Time to stop living in the past or future and join in the dance.

Can't escape

Life is now

Nowhere else

Can't get away, from the now.

Head in a phone

Dreaming of the past

Thinking of the future

You're doing it now.

This is it, all is now,

We all share in it

None can escape,

The here and now,

Young or old,

Rich or poor,

We all breathe now,

Life is now.

We all are equal

Under the sun.

This is it, be aware

Heaven is here and now.

Let it go

Can you grab the past?

Touch it, feel it, show your friends?

Or is it just in the mind,

Nowhere to be found,

Only comes to life, by our thoughts?

Gets stirred up by people we see,

Places we go, and what we remember,

Just as the wind makes the ocean dance.

If we look around, life it does not get stuck in the past.

Trees say bye to their leaves,

Birds are born, then fly away,

Flowers bloom then slowly fade,

All around is constant change.

Life happens now, there is no past

Flow with the now, and see the

Miracle that life is.

I am nothing

Life it moves along,

Marches on and on,

Day it, turns to night.

Spring it slowly turns to summer,

The tide comes in then out again,

Clouds they form, and rain pours down,

Each and every moment is brand new.

Who or what am I in all this?

Am I a doer of anything?

The spirit that moves all along

Is in me I do believe.

The spirit that beats my heart is the same spirit

That makes it rain, all is done for me.

I am nothing, but I am everything.

Old to new

No need to worry, like others may,

Jump from the old you, into the new.

Don't cling onto what's coming through,

All has gone, life is now.

Forget all you think you know,

See the world as a child,

Rediscover the wonder and joy of life.

Life is short, do not forget,

Don't hope for a future, which might not be;

Start now, do not delay.

Each moment of life is a new beginning,

See the wonder that life is

Here and now.

Future?

Do I have a future?

When all is said and done

How can this be

When I'm going to go?

Nothing is forever, that's how it is,

Just like the past

Is just in the mind.

Nowhere to be found,

This word, that we call future,

Only exists as a thought.

All there is and ever has been

Is this moment now.

Life does not start anywhere else,

No hope for a future,

Only hope we have is this present moment.

It's all we have, and when fully aware

You will find heaven right here,

On this earth we call home.

A mindful prayer

Great spirit of all life
I give thanks for this moment,
The only moment there is.
Help me to be aware, and feel alive in the moment,
To not live in the past, to be aware of the now.
Be with me so I will not worry about the future,
So I am able to see the miracle that is now.
When my mind is not in the present moment,
Uncertainty and confusion are with me.
Help me to keep my mind in the moment,
The place where peace can be found.
Great spirit of all life
Thank you for this moment,
The only moment that there is;
It is the place I can never leave,
Life is so much better when I am aware.

Light

How can I judge another without looking in the mirror?

Look at myself, long and hard:

Actions done, thoughts I have thought,

Am I better than the other?

We all are light, deep inside

But we live in the shade.

Find the light within, don't judge another,

For light will chase the shadows away

Only this moment

Only in this moment can I be,

Nowhere else am I.

When aware, no problems are there,

Only peace in the now.

Lost in thought and not aware,

The peace it walks away.

Stay aware of the now,

The place you can never leave, and peace will rule your heart.

Be still

Just be still,

Nothing to do,

Universe inside of you.

Stop being busy,

Give mind a rest,

Back to the self,

Source of all life.

That place we are from,

All is one,

That's how it is

When you be still.

Don't fight

Feel so restless and disturbed,

Far away from the place of peace.

Mind like a stormy sea, tossed and thrown by events of the world.

I will not fight you restless mind, will only make it worse,

Walk outside I hear kids at play, feel the wind on my skin,

Washing blowing on the line, flies bob and fly about.

Sit down and take a breath, peace within here again,

Mind has settled down; all I did was not resist.

A simple cup of Tea

Switching on the kettle, I am here aware of the now,

The steam it rises, up into the sky it goes, to maybe make a cloud and fall as rain.

I notice my hands as I take my cup, the patterns and lines like a tree trunk so fine.

The humming of the water as it boils, a robin joins in sounds of distant cars, pure sound such delight

The filling of the empty cup, the rising steam on its journey home, smell of tea, a warm glow on my face.

Sit down, take a breath, the sound of the robin, nature's heaven, no need for questions – just take a sip,

Feels like my first cup of tea, life is so simple when you're aware.

Eden

The space between thoughts

Is the place where Eden grows.

Away from mind,

Confusion and pain,

Stay in the garden of your soul.

Watch the flowers grow,

The place of peace,

Rest for our souls,

Its the best place for us to be.

The way

Sometimes a simple smile is best,

Words can lead to places of unrest.

Talk of the past or what's on the news

May leave the other dazed and confused.

Words stir emotions, like the wind shakes the tree,

So watch what you say to the people you see;

Sometimes a smile or hug is the way.

Storms

The storms they do rage, panic and fear are everywhere,

Choppy waters in the world of man,

Division, mistrust, love on the run,

Problems with yourself in your house, and in the world we live,

There always is, and will be, something going on.

Hard to find peace in the world made by man,

But if you stop and look around at this moment now,

Life it moves along, the birds they sing their song, eyes they blink, heart it beats;

Life is always good now no matter what we are going through,

Be aware of the moment and all will be well,

Panic and fear will come to an end.

Can we judge?

The stranger that we meet,

Drunken fool in the street,

The strange one at our work,

Friends and family that we have, husband or wife

And all that we see in this short but beautiful life,

How would we act if we had the genetics and life experiences of the other?

Can we truly judge another?

Live life

Life is so short

Can't let it pass you by.

Who and what we are?

There is no one who knows,

Don't take it too seriously,

Life it just happens to all of us.

We are not king of the world,

Just food for the worms at the end.

Don't take it too seriously,

Life it comes then it goes,

One shot its all you got,

Everyday could be your last.

Tricked myself

Fooled myself again, believing this moment should be changed, that it is ordinary and does not fit with what I want.

A pesky fly keeps on annoying me, won't go away, buzz off, leave me alone I'm trying to play on my phone.

The fly is stubborn, won't go away, lands on my arm, walks on my hairs, feels tickly now I'm aware.

Look at the eyes and patterns on its back, its perfect little wings,

I hear the birds, another fly it appears, this moment is new all that there is, never ordinary or boring;

The eternal moment here for us all, we just need to be aware.

Peace

Sit down take a breathe,

Feel the earth below your feet,

Ignore the thoughts, in your mind,

Deeply listen to all you hear,

Let go of any fear,

Take another long slow breathe,

Watch thoughts come and go,

Peace is now here with you,

The best feeling of them all.

This is it

This is it now, become aware,

Leave your mind alone,

Free yourself, from your greatest enemy,

Which is your own self,

Everything you've ever wanted,

Is here now,

All that you have searched for all these years,

Is here now.

Give it all up, to this moment now

Eternity is at your door,

All you need is to be aware.

Doubt

Doubt is here once more,

Tripped me up again.

Feeling unworthy and insecure,

Emotions from the past, stirred as wind stirs the water on a lake,

Telling me I'm no good and fake.

What is this voice inside my head?

Don't want to listen to you anymore,

You've started to become a bore.

I am not what people see, so much more universe inside of me,

I am in all that I see, and all I see is me;

Nice to be free from the voice within.

In the garden

In the unstoppable moment
Wind blowing washing on the line,
Dog is jumping, gift of life,
Sun, it hides behind a cloud,
Wind it tires and has a rest,
Foxglove turns a darker green,
Sparrows appear, then gone again,
Light of sun here once more,
The Buddha's head calm and still,
In our ever-changing world.

What am I

Who or what I am in this moment, does anyone know?

Name given at birth, flesh made of the earth, job that I work, Dad that I am, husband or son, brother, owner of dogs, lover of nature, drinker of tea or none of the above.

All of these are words made by man, and don't exist in the nature we see,

So, in this moment now, when feeling still and mind is at rest,

I feel that I am nothing in particular, no label or thing, and my mind is like space which contains everything.

Words and ideas have led me astray from the world that is me,

In stillness I return to the love that I am

Born equal

All are born equal so they say, but is true?

Spend our lives getting told what to do.

Some are above, at the top-

Big houses, fancy cars, money fame and power,

While those at the bottom want to get to the top.

Some even have no place to live,

Government's make laws to keep you down,

One law for rich, another for the poor,

Put you in a box, white, black, working class, 1st world people, on and on it goes.

If all are born equal, then how can this be?

Because this is the world, of man that you see,

There is another world at play, invisible to most,

We're all are equal, under the sun, and we have rights given to us by the creator of life,

We all need air and water to drink, food to eat and somewhere to live,

Freedom to move, and live as we choose,

We all are made of this great earth, where none is greater than the other,

The same spirit that turns night into day, is moving all along to the beat of its drum.

Just remember when you get told what to do, or you feel so small worthless and all,

That nobody is greater than you, only in mans world is this true,

The great illusion from when we were born; but in the world of nature great spirit of life,

We all are equal under the sun.

The best

We all want to be happy,

Want the best for ourselves,

Forever searching, in this world,

For peace, joy and happiness.

But just as the tree is in the seed,

Happiness is already, in all of us,

No need to look, for what's already there!

Experience

Life is an experience, not to be missed,

To special to waste even one day,

Could get the call at any time,

To meet your maker, be blown away.

Every second of everyday,

Is a real experience, an encounter with life,

To precious to waste, lost in our minds,

When all around, life marches on,

Try not to miss, your time on this earth.

Free

Sitting here being still,

They can never get to me,

For I am free here and now,

No chains can I see,

Only space that never ends,

So how can I be tied down?

When I am unbound and free,

Society tries to keep me down,

In a box, a separate thing,

But I am space, one with all,

Don't need to be told, that I am free.

You

Perfection is what you are,

Expression of the universe,

Don't believe, the words you think,

They keep you down, feeling small.

Time has come to take your place,

As child of this earth, alive and free,

Let go of the thoughts of old,

Say bye to all that's been,

Future can not be seen,

The only thing that remains,

Is this moment now,

Pure perfection is what you are.

My world

I look at my world,

The world I see and feel,

It is myself, ancient I am.

My hands are like rocks,

Feet are the ground that I walk.

Trees are my air, a tree I am,

Bees buzzing, noise made by me.

My world is me, and I am my world,

That's the way it is when I'm aware.

Only now

There is only now

Nothing else can there be,

A flea lands on me,

Cloud covers the sun,

Feeling cold

The cloud it goes,

Feeling warm

Life moves on,

All happens now.

Let it all go

The only time is now,

Yesterday has gone away,

Tomorrow is all in the mind.

Let life come to you,

Don't fight what's coming through,

Let go and you will find

The universe inside of you.

Sitting still

Sitting down trying to be still,

Hand it moves to bite a nail,

Reaches for the phone

Scratching head, playing with hair,

Mind it races here and there,

Itching skin, touching face,

Go to grab phone again.

This is hard, this sitting still.

The howling wind, it draws me in,

Fish in tank, swim about,

Tiny flies in front of me,

Mind feels calm, peace is here,

Not so bad, this sitting still.

Ignore

If I try to fight you, mind,

The only thing I will find

Is that you can't be beaten by force;

Fighting will only give life to my thoughts,

Problems they will arise,

Best to keep watch and try to ignore,

Listen to what the world has to say,

Then like the earth after the storm

Calmness it will return, and peace will be here once more.

Forever here

Just here is all that I am

No matter where it is, that I may be

I am always here.

Look outside for peace of mind,

Could travel the world only to find that

I am here.

Could be in pain, or in the rain, on a mountain summer's day.

On a busy city street, watching people go on their way,

No matter where it is that I may be, can never get away from myself,

Or the fact that I am here, and nowhere else can I be.

Missing out

Me on a chair, fully aware,

Dog chewing bone, kid on a phone,

Grinding teeth, dog's delight, sun so bright

Kid he moans that he can't see the phone,

Nettles turning to seed, so beautiful and green,

Sun so hot, off comes my top.

Hear a moan about wi-fi,

Flies buzz past my ear, sound of water down the drain,

Dogs panting, they are in heaven,

Dandelion seed floats on by, dancing fairy in the sky,

Kid's eye not left the phone

A walk

I went for a walk,

Didn't want to talk,

Had enough of words;

What are they about?

Too much talking, thinking,

Found a track surrounded by trees,

Now I am here, feel I can breathe.

Like another realm, all is now still,

All feels slow, this is not time.

Feel so alert, can see through the world,

Go back to house, still alert as before,

This feeling that I have, is forever there,

Does not matter where I am,

All that matters is being aware,

Awareness will chase the doubts away.

Bye Bye

Bored of it all:

Habits of a lifetime

Thinking the thoughts,

Speaking the words,

Buying the stuff,

Watching the films,

Eating the junk,

Judging another,

Gossip and the slander,

Playing with phones,

Had enough of the voice inside my head.

Time to say 'bye bye' to the voice inside,

Nice to have known you

But it's time to go back to my natural state.

The sneer

What is that when I see another,

The little sneer to myself?

Judging appearance, or clothes they wear, before I even say 'hello'.

Where does this come from, this snigger from within,

Has it always been there?

At least now I'm aware, I can see others as they are,

Not as I think they should be.

The problem is with me, not the other

Look at myself first, before sneering at another.

Not about me

Too long I thought it was all about me

Walking through life in my own private dream,

Deeply intimate separate from all,

Only I had the key to the world made by me.

Cut off from nature source of all life,

Living in a make believe world,

As my mind became still, and new light it shone in,

Could finally see it's not about me.

Old beliefs were blown away,

Awoke to the oneness all around,

My world is now open, and me has gone away.

Nothing

From thinking that the world it revolves around me,

To the feeling I am nothing, no thing at all;

Just a babe in a pram, flowing through life

No destination to reach, just the journey of now,

Have no requirements of life, nothing that I need?

From dust I came, to dust I shall return,

Take what comes with humble heart, seeing love in all I meet,

Nothing has been lost on the way,

But gained it all because the world is me.

Good to think?

Is it good to think?

Good to have thoughts And to wonder on things to come?

A million possibilities for every situation.

Our minds only get in the way; what ifs and maybes

Tying our minds in knots, stirring up feelings and emotions.

Does a swallow think, and plan its voyage home?

Get in a state of worry and dread? Or do they get a feeling deep within,

A knowing and a trust in the universe?

Do we spend too much time in the head, and not enough in the heart?

Play

Children at play, time is at bay,

Lost in the moment, not worried by next,

Five hours could pass, may seem like one.

A different world than the one on the news,

No thought of future or what's been and gone,

Pure imagination, why can't it last?

Grow up so fast, get caught by the world

Like a bird in a cage lost in a maze,

The child has never left us, with us still now

When we forget the world and follow our hearts.

Sacred

No such thing as ordinary,

For it is where the holy is found;

Majestic trees and bumble bees,

Tiny seeds grow to food we eat,

The people we see in our day,

Acts of love big and small,

Don't be fooled by familiar things,

Be aware and you may see the sacred everywhere.

Chapter 2
Nature

Reflect

Gulls flying over still, calm water,

The sea does not choose to reflect, but reflect the gull it does.

Choppy waters, stormy seas, reflection you will not see;

Only when peace is there will the sea reflect.

You and I are here to reflect the love from where we came,

When we are mad or anger it stirs, love does not reflect;

Only when we are still and calm do we reflect the love that we are.

Patch

Patch of nettles so beautiful and green

Reveal to me my true nature,

Beyond the forms and labels

The world of this and that,

Invisible realm, open to all,

Touched from time to time, in high moments of life,

On a beach or alone on a hill,

Way beyond the body and the mind

There is so much more for us to find.

Sparrow

A tiny sparrow on a tree,

In my garden on the street,

Me in the kitchen, cooking food,

Far away from mountains, and temples,

Me and the sparrow, eye to eye,

All that I know, has gone away,

The hand of time, has waved goodbye,

Now is all that there is.

I could read books forever,

Search for the meaning of life,

Meditate for hours and hours,

Have knowledge, of the religions of the world.

Only to find, the divine in my kitchen,

In what we call ordinary life.

Magic

Magic is all around,

Little seed in the ground,

From the dark into the light,

How it happens I don't know.

Little sun, little rain, bit of wind now and then,

Guided by the invisible hand

That loves and nourishes all the land,

And performs its magic for all to see;

Don't be fooled by the modern world,

The real magician waves his wand, can't be seen,

But the magic is all around.

Stay

Stay with nature through your day,

For it is the royal way,

Fantasising about this and that, only leads you astray.

The love inside the egg, before it is hatched,

Is the same love that was with you inside your mother's womb.

The love from nature is for all,

Your days are joyful when you walk with this love.

It's so easy to forget, and get lost in the world

But nature and the love are always around.

Eyes up

Lift up your eye,

Look to the skies,

Makes you calm and still.

Problems will arise,

It's the nature of life,

But don't seem so bad

When your eyes are on the skies,

Rest

Trees they rest in the evenness of now,

Seem content with what comes their way.

Howling wind, trees they bend,

Perfectly still when the wind is no more.

Soak in the rain, do not complain,

Leaves they come and go.

Burning sun, magical frost

Glowing in the light of the moon.

Never will you hear a tree moan,

Completely at rest in nature's breast,

Not trying to be something that it is not.

Which one?

The sea reflecting in the eyes of a gull,

Such beauty and mystery,

Turns its head, a bank is now reflecting in its eyes

The world of money and of greed,

We all carry these within us all

Which one will we choose?

The return

Return of the wind,

I've missed you dear friend,

Sounds of trees and rustling leaves,

The feel of you on my face.

Where have you been, mysterious one

While we have basked in the glorious sun?

Trees so still, nothing has moved,

A deafening silence, calm and so still,

And now you are here, wind so dear,

To make our world dance, and to wake us from trance

And feel the mystery that you are.

All done

What is it that I do?

Summer follows spring,

Winter follows autumn,

The tide it comes in, then out again.

Plants they grow, wind it blows,

Sun, it shines, and rain pours down.

Do I breathe or grow my nails?

Beat my heart, pump my blood?

All is done by an invisible hand,

Guiding all that we see.

Everything is done for me,

I am just a happy nothing on a journey through this life.

Become

From the womb to walking the earth,

Caterpillar to butterfly,

Acorn seed to mighty oak,

Miracles they are everywhere.

When we become aware,

We ourselves become a miracle.

Look into the mirror, and you may see

A miracle starring back at you.

Mr Bee

Looking at you Mr bee,

What's the space between you and me?

Moving along to the rhythm of life,

No worries about the hand of time,

Alive in the moment, at one with the flower,

Work is done then back to the hive.

Don't want no thanks, or pat on the back

Take no credit for a job well done,

Day is over memories, they are gone.

You are not worried by what tomorrow may bring,

Alive in the eternal now are you Mr bee.

All will pass

Day it follows, the night,

Calm will follow, the storm,

Spring will never be,

Without the cold winter chill,

Clouds they will disappear,

The sun will reappear.

No matter what you are going through,

It will always pass, if you let it flow,

Nature forever follows,

Its heavenly course.

Looking at me

Pigeon walking on the land,

I am sitting by the sand,

Who's doing the looking, me or you?

Sea is calm, like my mind

Could there be just one eye, looking out from the sky?

Is it so that you and me, and all we see,

Are God in drag, acting out our worldly roles?

Teatime

Been here a thousand times before,

Cutting and chopping for my tea,

Boring or ordinary it may be,

But not for those with eyes to see.

Takes me beyond my tiny mind,

Away from this kitchen of mine,

Cutting beetroot, cabbage, onions and broccoli,

I can see the world in front of me.

Patterns like rocks that live by the sea, drops of rain making ripples as they hit the water, beautiful trees, lovely and green, one tiny piece can recreate the whole, vivid colours – reds and green, white like the snow full of nature's glow,

Shapes and patterns, spiral's galore, no human could make, only nature could produce this fine art.

I am not alone chopping my veg, for the whole world is here with me.

Little seed

Break forth out of your shell

From the dark world below,

To the light the world above.

Become what you are meant to be,

Nothing else, pure and free,

No holding on, let life come,

Let the world know that you are

With patience and trust, and knowledge of self,

Little seed you will become a mighty tree.

Solid

Branches shaken by the wind,

Shadows dancing, on the ground,

Leaves they are blowing, everywhere,

Movement, it is all around,

Except for the trunk, so stable and strong,

Rooted deep in the earth, not shaken by the world,

Remaining calm in the fiercest storm,

The storms of life, will rock you to,

Troubles will knock at your door,

It is the nature, of this life,

Better to be like, the trunk of the tree,

Rooted in the earth, stable and strong,

Than like the branches, not being in control, when this life it gets rough.

Open

A rose will open when the time is right,

Guided by the spirit of light,

Does not force, lets life come,

Complete trust in the universe.

If the flower opens too soon

The full glory won't be seen.

We all will flower when the time is right,

Flow with nature with all your might.

Perfect

Seashell, oh Seashell,

On the seashore,

Oh, so perfect, just as you are,

Nothing to change, nothing to add,

So it is with you and me, and all that we see,

We all are perfect just as we are.

Alone

Are we ever truly alone?

Little spider in my room,

Invisible air so I can breathe,

Chatter of birds brings me joy,

Little moth, by the light,

Life it keeps moving on;

It is always there with you.

Blackbird

The day has dawned,

I hear your song again,

A sound beyond time

Too beautiful for words.

Awake, or do I dream

This sound so divine?

Full circle I have come,

For dusk it has arrived,

Blink of an eye, back to start,

Noise from heaven here again.

Your sound, it fills me up,

Takes me beyond, my wondering mind,

More than just a blackbird you are to me.

Greed

Why is there so much greed

When nature has all we need?

Competition desires, wrong ideas

Keep us away from who we are.

All are equal under the sun,

The moon shines on everyone.

Bank accounts, status and wealth, houses, cars and material stuff,

Keep you believing in a separate self.

Look to nature and you will see

There is only so much that we need,

And in no other species will you see greed.

Duality

Ladybird in the sun,

Cricket in the shade,

Snail on the ground,

Falcon up above.

One day happy.

Next day sad,

Soft skin,

Majestic rock,

Peacock in full display,

Slug gliding on the floor,

Busy high street,

Lonely desert,

Inside my skull,

World outside,

Can't have one without the other.

Grow

From out of the winter,

Comes the spring,

Death has occurred,

Life can now grow

Like Christ on the cross.

Death is our friend,

The seed, it must die

To become what it is.

Sit

Sitting, looking and listening,

Gentle breeze on my skin.

Cherry blossom petal falls to the ground,

Tiny fly says 'hello',

Army of ants under my feet,

Sounds of traffic, taking flight,

Buzz of a bee, cry of a gull,

Dandelion with its bright yellow glow.

Talking people pass on their way,

Spiders web, just for me.

A few moments have passed, that is all

How could we ever call life dull?

Trance

Wind it howls,

Dogs do growl,

Waves that talk,

Seagulls squawk,

Snails go slow,

Flowers they glow,

Flies do their dance,

Humans walking in a trance.

Little fly

Little fly zig zagging about,
Living your life as it's meant to be lived,
Alive in the moment, no cares or regrets,
Not worried by next, status or wealth.
Playing with the rhythms of life,
Just being a fly and nothing else
Made so perfect, has all that you need
To live a full life, here and now.

On the edge

Jackdaw baby on a ledge,

Life very much on the edge.

On a busy city street

People sipping coffee, unaware what's up above.

Mother brings food with love,

Cars on their furious flight,

Baby flaps its wings, with all its might.

Will you fly when you jump,

And be free to soar up in the sky?

Or dodging traffic in the street,

Life is always on the edge.

Life in motion

In a garden oh so small,

Seems like a portal to a world beyond,

Talking flies on my mind,

Whispering ants to be found,

Babies in roofs, wanting food.

Mothers flying back and forth,

Bees in flowers for their queen,

Light so bright, foxgloves delight,

Floating mountain now shade is here,

Grass it turns a darker green

Phone it rings, brings me back to the material world.

Let go

Out of the depths of the cold silence

From the dark, of what we call winter,

To the light and warmth of the spring,

Comes new life, and hope for all.

Winter does not hold on; it lets go and flows into the spring

Just as the day flows into night, and spring into the summer,

Then why should we hold on to all that happens to us?

When all around, nature teaches us to let go, and not hold on

So we can let the miracle of life flow through us

The chase

Walking dog on a coastal cliff

Sheep appear, chase is on.

Dog and sheep heading for the sea,

Close my eyes, fingers crossed,

Sheep jump to a ledge,

Dog stops on the edge,

Heart in mouth, dog comes back,

Moment gone forgotten, by dog

Don't get stuck in the past, be like the dog and let it go.

Cause and effect

Wind moves a pile of leaves,

Dog jumps, tries to catch.

Kids leave food in a park,

Screaming seagulls swoop with speed.

Pigeon feathers fall to earth,

Falcon flying up above.

Mind is still and at ease,

Feeling calm full of peace.

My soul

Oh, my soul, my pure delight!

Joy within, the garden of my heart

In bloom once more,

Full of colour and light, a light so bright shines for all,

Weeds of my heart have withered away,

Only peace remains, and love for all.

Heaven and earth

Clouds they move up above,
Shadows glide across the ground,
Birds float way out there,
Seagull's dance, worms they rise,
Moon lights up the star-lit night,
Hedgehogs emerge, full of grace.
Thunder roars its heavenly tune,
Trees sway and bob about;
Drops of rain fall with speed,
Nourish and love all the land.
Heaven up above, earth below,
Between the two my life flows.

Hidden

Just as food is hidden in the seed,

The divine is to be found deep within me.

Plant myself in the earth, trust in nature, not in the man-made world.

Let life come, don't resist; thankful for all that comes my way.

Don't complain, need it all, sun and the rain,

And in due time I will flower, and the bees will come to me.

Ghost

Hawk, like a ghost, gliding by my side,

Carry on down the track; light it turns to shade,

Feathers floating silently through the air,

Walk on, the sun appears again.

Little robin

Little robin, why do you make such beautiful noise?

Surely not from instinct or a warning call to rivals, both big and small.

Does it come from the depths of your being, from your beautiful soul?

And you sing for the love of song, and to bring wonder and joy to all.

The last leaf

Oh, little leaf you are the last to fall,

All of your friends have fallen and been scattered by the wind,

Back into the ground, to nourish the soil and feed your friend, the tree.

Don't hang on to this life you now live; let go and have no fear,

For when you fall it is not the end, back to the tree you will go.

The rays of the sun's energy you did catch, and sent it into the tree,

You've seen it all come and go, the flowers the fruits,

The birds who made their home in your friend, the tree.

You danced in the light of the moon and stars, the wind and the rain, you loved them all.

And now on this cold, December day, it's time for you to float away

Back to the tree, from where you came, and it is thank you from me,

And all mankind, for you are the reason that we breathe.

Chapter 3
Love

Walk in love

Walk in love today,

Do all that needs to be done

With love in your heart.

Walk in love, greet all in love,

If someone is cruel, or mean to you

Keep hold of the love, just walk on.

We are so much better when love is there,

The world feels different, more alive.

Love is the best part of us all,

Keep hold of the love, and don't be afraid.

Pure

Every heart is pure and kind,

Some have been underused,

Not been shown how to love,

Heart of gold turned to rust,

Act with love to all you meet,

For love will clean the rust away.

Fields of love

How can I be unkind to any living being when the world is myself?

From love I grew and back to love I will go;

All is love that we see, but some got lost along the way.

Nothing is greater than the other,

All has grown from fields of love.

Take a look and you will find

The world you see is you and me.

Suckle

Lambs suckling milk from mothers' plate,

Dog goes wild on owner's return,

Gull swoops to protect its nest,

A baby feeds on mothers' breast,

Bees gather pollen for their queen,

Man helps drunk to his feet,

Friends they hug when they meet,

Love it happens, all around,

May seem small, but love can heal one and all.

Float

Float like a cloud

Away from your mind,

And into boundless love.

Away from fears, pain and regrets,

Pure love waits for you.

A love beyond your tiny mind,

Which loves just a few;

But a love for all that you see

On your journey through life,

When you float away.

Mother earth

No divisions will you see in our mother earth,

Maps and countries are from the minds of man,

Nationalities, races and colours are giving to us at our birth-

None of this is real in our mother nature.

We all came from the one, and like a glass bottle thrown in the air

And shattered into millions of pieces, we have been divided from each other,

And our mother, who misses us so dear.

The journey back home is easier than you think;

We all are born from love and love is what we are,

All we see is connected, like the blood that unites one and all,

Every heart that beats, echoes all the hearts in the world,

And our mother's heart moves all of life along.

The eyes that we see day by day are the eyes of the world,

Nothing ever stands alone; division is only in the mind.

No wonder there is anger and fear, hate and mistrust,

When we have moved away from our mother's care.

All violence and depression, anger and greed, will melt away

When we find the love that we are;

Then Eden, will be here once more.

Nourish

Love and nourish your soul, take care of yourself,

Let peace grow and flourish within,

A peace to take you through this life.

Not getting dragged into its drama

Stops you reacting to outer events,

But makes you stable and strong like the biggest tree

Rooted in the earth, not shaken by the world.

Be with yourself, feed your soul well,

Turn away from negative things,

Make peace within, and peace will rule your heart.

Imagine

Imagine a place, a place of love

Where nothing ever goes wrong,

That does not change, even though we age,

Forever remains the same.

In times of trouble, heartache or loss,

Pure love is close at hand;

A love beyond the world, a refuge from it all,

Always there for you;

A love beyond your name, body and form and

What people say you are.

This place of love, is not very far, closer than you dare believe;

It's in our souls, never complaining, patiently waiting

For us to dive within, and drown in the ocean of love

Surrender

As water, finds its lowest point

On its way back to the source,

So it is with us, when despair and anguish close in

We hit rock bottom, we are at the source, the place of love.

Waiting for us to surrender, get on our knees and give up all we know,

As water finds its way back to the sea

We find the love that gave birth to all.

Open

I am here to open up to the love that I am,

Too long my door was closed,

Only loving those close to me, and even to them the love was cold.

Being held back by my mind,

Scared to let go, closed I was,

Became bored, with the thoughts that I had

Started to see life as it is, and not as I wanted it to be,

Seeing and experiencing, the oneness of the world

My door is now open, and I am drowning in an ocean of love

For one and all.

Nothing without love

You can have it all, that this world has to offer:

Cars, toys, money and fame

Friends, family, house in the sun,

But if you do not have love for all, and love deep in your soul,

Then what do you have?

Easy to love who you know;

Can you love strangers in the street?

Easy to love when all is well;

But when times are hard?

Easy to love when you get what you want;

Do you love when you don't?

Love divine is in us all,

A love so pure and true

Asks for nothing, keeps on giving.

Love the world as yourself,

Care for all, friends and foe,

Then love divine will come knocking at your door;
You will then truly have it all.

Deep

Plant seeds of love and happiness,

Live in harmony,

All is one,

Under the sun,

Stop being on the run,

Find out what you are,

Not what people say,

But what you are deep in your core,

Love it can show you the way,

To what you truly are.

Without

Without love

Nothing would grow,

No sun would shine,

No one would dance,

Smiles would be frowns,

We all would be down,

No babies born.

Would we be here

Without love?

Grows

Love, it grows and grows,

Hate tears down and destroys.

Love, it heals one and all,

Hate, it makes your body old.

Love unites all mankind,

Hate divides and separates.

Love it spreads everywhere,

Hate destroys all who hate.

Chose love over hate

For it is our natural state.

With love

Little sparrow,

Back and forth you go

To the place

Where the babies grow,

Giving everything, you have.

Act of love,

Pure and kind,

Never stopping for a rest

Till your babies

Have flown the nest.

Come home

All we do, all we say

Keeps us away, from the love we are:

Always moving, seeking and looking

Plotting and planning

For a tomorrow that may never come.

Take it all away: the titles, names and clothes,

The toys, fears and desires, beliefs and ideas.

What is it that's left of this life you have built?

One day, who knows when, the time has come

To go to the great beyond, and leave this life behind.

All we have built will be destroyed,

None can escape this fact.

Don't get to the end without touching

The unlimited reservoir of love within;

Spending our days, looking outside,

When the treasure has been us the whole time.

Maybe too simple for our inquisitive minds

But simple is always best.

Chapter 4
Live life give thanks

Thank you

Two small words to say every day

Not very hard, to say

For the gift of life.

The birds and the trees,

Family and friends, and people we meet,

For the sun in the sky and all we receive, good and bad.

If you can only say one prayer this day

Let it be thank you!

Our choice

We choose to be happy.

On a warm summers day

The wind is no more, and children do play,

Sun on our skin, so warm and so new,

Smell of the flowers, buzz of the bees.

This feeling is within and never outside,

So don't be too sad when the sun goes away,

Just choose to be happy when skies they are grey.

Your peace

Don't let anything steal your peace today –
Not the weather, a nasty look from a stranger,
A memory from the past
Or the headlines in the news.
Its your peace, let what comes flow through,
Don't hold on and let anger rise up,
Keep watch try not to react,
Keep your peace, enjoy this day.

Star

Trust in yourself, and nothing else;

You are the one who is always there,

You are not what people say,

So much more – a shining star.

Learn to love who you are,

You are one with all that you see,

Expression of this universe

Pure and so free.

Freedom

Talk about freedom;

Freedom from this, freedom from that,

Free, to go here, free to go there,

Free to do what I want,

Free to not give a!!!!

Freedom lost, freedom gained,

Free to love who you choose;

But do you truly know that we are

Free right here, right now,

A freedom within that can't be taken away

 By anything in society.

Look within and you will find

The true freedom that you are.

Annoyed

Waking up, cold frosty day,

Thinking of holidays and clothes to buy,

Worried by events going on in the world.

Get up, get changed, belts on the wrong way,

Feel annoyed, anger it stirs; make some coffee,

Get lost in a phone, coffee cold,

Bad mood on the rise.

Rude to a girl in the shop,

People that I see are bothering me.

Different shapes and sizes, judgemental thoughts fill my head –

Get a job, state of you, ever heard of fresh food.

Think of the world and how long will it last,

Feel anxious, not flowing with life;

Back to my bed at the end of the day.

Wake up, hear the rain hitting the window,

Sound of the wind and cry of the gulls,

Go to grab phone but leave it alone,

Give thanks for my life and all that I have.

Float down the stairs, listen to a robin as he awakens my soul,

Sipping my coffee as the wind talks to me,

Give thanks for life again, smile at a man I see on the street,

Love is here, love all that I meet; rain pours down,

I don't care - I am thankful for just being alive.

Taps

We are all the same, me and you,

However, we may disagree.

We all came from this earth;

Like a bulb in the soil, we grow, then we flower,

All differences are in our minds,

Which keeps us alone and afraid,

Believing that we live in a world that does not care,

A world of survival and strongest win out,

Different races and colours;

But if our minds were like taps

That could be turned off,

What would be left?

Stillness and peace, and a mind like space,

A oneness with all big and small.

Who knows?

How are we here, is there any that know?
Clever people say we came from a bang,
A single source that gave birth to the world.
People of faith say we all came from God
Who created the heavens and the earth we call home?
Wise people say all is vibration
The dance of sound and vibration brought all of this about;
All words and ideas from afar,
The only thing you know is that you are.
I am not clever or wise,
Just a fool who knows I am not separate from all that I see,
Don't need to know, the who, why, what or where,
Just a knowing deep within, that I am here –
Always have been, and I will be forevermore.

Unite

Why do we have to fight?

It's so much easier to unite.

Life can be tough, but we make it so much tougher

When we fight with each other.

How can we judge another before looking in the mirror?

Hate, jealously, fear and anger

Use up so much of our energy, and spread negativity into the world,

When peace and love are so natural and free,

To love each other is the way we are meant to go,

Sharing this blessed gift of life with each other;

We breathe the same air, so let's share the love

With each, and unite with our brothers and sisters.

The gift

To wake up each and every day and be me,

Is it the greatest gift of them all?

Better than any experience that the world can offer

Living in a system, which tells you that you're no good,

That life has no meaning, just keep on working, paying your taxes

Worshipping footballers and actors, makers of music

People with yachts and banks full of cash,

Always comparing yourself, never seeing yourself as you are.

But this is not the way it should be

For we are divine, what else can we be?

My eyes are the greatest jewels you will ever see,

They give life to the world; would the world be here without me?

These ears of mine evoke sound from the earth,

They give life to the greatest sounds of them all.

Each moment I am here is so unique, once in a lifetime won't come again,

Life is a miracle and so are we.

Don't ever pretend that life is ordinary and you're no good,

When you are the universe, what else could you be?

Be light

Keep your humanity while others lose theirs,

Shine your light as the world turns dark,

Keep your peace, as others get bitter and full of rage,

Have no fear, just have the courage of life,

Don't bow down to authority, stand up for your rights, question it all,

Offer a smile, when no one else does,

Don't let the system drag you down,

Be the love that you are, don't let hate take over your soul.

Watching

Watching the rain pouring down,

Hitting the puddles on the ground,

Ripples, they are all around.

People running like the world is ending,

It wasn't long ago that the sun was shining in full glow,

Deep blue sky, smell of flowers in the air,

Some were complaining it was just too hot,

But to a fool like me, watching puddles in the street,

Every day is sunshine inside of me and

There are miracles everywhere, no matter the weather.

Water

Where are you drinking the water to nourish your soul?

Do we drink the water of the modern world?

Or the life-giving water for our soul?

The water of the world will make you thirsty for more and more,

While the water for your soul will nourish your every need.

A win on the lottery will quench your thirst for a time,

But soon your thirst will come back again.

Promotion at work, new house or car, will make your thirst come back again,

Like the swallow who comes back to the place where he was born.

Only the water from the well of eternal life will satisfy your thirst

That no money can ever buy,

It's found in the depths of your soul, within your very being,

Waiting for you to take a sip, and you will never be thirsty again.

Best times

Why do we bother with what people think about us?

It only stops us from being our true selves.

The best times in life are when you are happy and free,

Without a care in the world, alive in the moment of life,

Singing your heart out in the shower, or falling in love,

Dancing in the mirror, with no thought of the world,

Just alive in the moment no problem to be found.

But when we are out in the world this energy is locked away,

Worried what people may think of us, our clothes, hair or shoes.

Don't worry what people may think, don't be afraid to hug a tree,

Rediscover the child within, carefree and living life without regret,

Being moved along by the pulse of life.

Grass

Next time you feel at your wits end, and life is getting you down,

When worry and fear has taken you over,

You can find help from an unlikely source.

You see it all the time; it becomes a chore in the summer months:

You walk on it, run on it, and sit down on it and it provides food for all,

But have you ever taken time to look at it?

There is a miracle all around us,

The beautiful green grass being blown by the wind,

Morning dew so pure and so fresh, it takes all that life throws without complaint.

The rain and wind, even snow, gets walked on and even cut,

But back it comes, again and again, never lying down when life gets tough.

Out comes the mower, back comes the grass,

It would be easy for the grass to stay down.

But its life in motion, to keep on going,

So next time you feel down or depressed,

Just remember you have a friend under your feet –

Beautiful green grass, tougher than you think,

Full of mystery and wonder when you look.

Royal

Kings walking around as beggars,

Heads down wearing frowns,

Not realising it should be a crown;

Believing in this the phony world,

Ignoring our heritage, ancient and old,

Spending days disappointed by life.

Walking around in a private dream,

Gripped by fears, and traumas of past.

Slow down oh kings, come and see

Your treasure within waiting for you.

We are richer and more powerful than we dare believe,

Not just a number in the world of man,

But royal and divine, nothing else could we be,

We are all kings, and the world is our kingdom.

What are you?

You are not a name or number, clothes you wear or job title,

You are not your school report from long ago that said you were a fool,

You are not what your friends or enemies say about you,

Or that boy or girl from long ago.

You are not your fear or stress, jealousy or hate;

You are not even the same person before reading this,

You are so much more than you dare to believe.

Dwelling place of the divine, child of the universe, limitless and free,

You are pure love and happiness, stronger than you think,

Take away your mind and what is there left?

Just the universe becoming conscious
 of itself.

Thought

For what is a thought, from where does it come?

What is this thing we call thinking?

A little voice inside our heads bobbing from one thing to the next,

Never stopping for a rest, constantly reacting to this and that,

Plotting, planning, dreaming, worries and fears judging others,

Does this voice ever rest?

It's been with us for so long we think it's normal,

But do the birds and trees have this voice inside like me?

Or are they at rest in each moment of life?

If the voice within never stops, how can we hear what the world has to say?

Locked in our own private world,

Not hearing the birds, and waves, wind and friends,

Chatter, chatter – on and on it goes like the ocean in a storm,

Currents and waves being thrown about against their will.

But what happens when you dive below the surface?

The waves are no more, and stillness is there.

Is it the same for us, when we stop running and look within ourselves?

Could we find peace in the depths of our being,

Free from the thoughts that keep us locked in our prison?

Our prison of fear and separateness from our world,

They only thing that separates us from the nature is this thing called thinking;

So, is it natural to think? Maybe, maybe not;

Sometimes it might be best, to simply sit and say nothing,

So the world can talk to us.

Now

Where do you live your life?

Are you on pause, rewind, or fast forward?

Do you live life on pause, going through the motions, asleep to the miracles which are around us and in us, lost in the routine of 9 to 5?

Or do you live life on rewind, living in the past, with all the regrets, guilt and what ifs?

Do you live life on fast forward, plotting and planning, for a future that may never come, worried by what may be, trying to manage things so they fall under you will?

There is another way to live life, and that is live life now,

All you need to do is stop, breathe and relax; what is going on now?

A leaf has just fallen from a tree; just for you, a stranger is standing next to you,

The universe has brought you together,

A robin is singing his song just for you.

You notice the trees so majestic and proud; you feel the wind on your face like an old friend saying 'hello'.

A rook appears; you notice the patterns and colours on it feathers, they are not just black meaningless things.

You feel alive and alert, then you stop frozen in time, you look up and notice the heavens, the sky, the clouds - everything seems brand new.

Have I been asleep all these years?

This is how it feels when you live life now.

Chapter 5
Death

Live

All going to go,

Beginning's the end.

Can't put it off,

May as well laugh.

Change is all around,

Nothing stays the same;

Bank full of money,

Can't take it with,

Its all just a game.

Stop playing, you will see

Life is now,

Nowhere else,

It's all a miracle,

Make every second count,

Because we are all going to

DIE.

Take the plunge

Why so scared, why so afraid?

Baby gull on a tall building,

Don't know if it will fly or fall,

Does, not think of life or death,

Takes the plunge, here we go;

Are we, scared of change?

Or afraid of the future?

Change is here, every second of every day,

Are we afraid of the future?

How can it be, when there are a million different outcomes for every situation?

Or do we really fear our comfortable little lives coming to an end,

The known, thinking this is how its going to be forevermore.

All around life comes, then goes,

Heartache, disappointment and loss are all part of life.

The unexpected is bound to happen, when plans and expectations can be taken away, before the next breath.

The meaning of this life is so simple and easy,

It is just to live and be alive, not to be scared and afraid.

Take it all with humble heart, and be like the gull,

Take the plunge, and dive into life.

In the air

Fear of death is in the air, can smell it everywhere,

Hanging over us like a cloud, makes you want to scream so loud,

If you fear death you are not alive,

And if you're not alive then you are dead.

Don't live life inside the head, look to the heart, open up.

From where I sit, death is good:

Spider's web, full of fly's, caterpillars on the flowers, seeds in soil, they must die.

Life and death is one and the same; better to die to your old self.

With death of the mind, you may find

The glory of life, right here right now.

Can't take it too seriously, be cause at the end,

I'm just food for the worms.

The way

We are all going to die,

That's how it is.

Why waste time

In negativity, and gossip?

Not much time, make it count,

Death is the way to free your mind,

Nothing is permanent

So why make plans?

Building your empire.

Its all going to crash,

The treasure's within,

Death will give you the key.

Titanic

Humanity is all aboard the good ship Titanic, p

Future uncertain, adventure of life,

Who knows what will be? Enjoy the ride while it lasts.

On a great voyage into the great unknown

Leave your baggage and troubles behind.

One way ticket, paradise awaits,

Live in the moment, embrace the journey,

Danger can strike at any time.

Don't get stuck in the routines and requirements of life:

Life is a miracle, sacred and divine, always alive and ever anew.

Storms will happen, hard times we will face,

Treat it all as a blessing, a gift from above,

No destination to reach, only the now.

Live every second, don't miss the wonder,

Enjoy the journey, let's make it a blast.

www.ingramcontent.com/pod-product-compliance
Lightning Source LLC
Chambersburg PA
CBHW030908080526
44589CB00010B/199